THE
REDEMPTION HOUSE

RACHEL HAGGERTY

INTRODUCTION

As you read this book, you will go on a journey with me through a time of my life when I faced the hardest obstacles I've ever had to face. You will see me fail and fall short as a wife, mother of three and daughter of God. But you'll also see throughout this whole book how our Heavenly Father proved Himself faithful.

You will see me stand up, fighting tooth and nail for peace and joy to be mine again. You will get to know my family, just as we are, without things being hidden or covered up. You will laugh with me and cry tears of sadness and of joy.

If there is one thing you get out of this book and the story of my life, I hope it is that God loves you, not in the way you can imagine in your mind but in the mystery of His unimaginable care for you. In this you would find how He loves every part of the perfect human he made you to be.

You will begin reading about my life living on a farm in an antique farmhouse built in the 1800s. My diary entries of that time are included after each chapter about living on the farm. This is so that you know what I was going through on a deeper level as I was learning how to cope with the horror that I faced everyday living in that house.

I bless your mind, body and soul as you read about mine.

CHAPTER 1:

The musty smell overcame my senses as I walked into the farmhouse. I had been there before, but this time it was mine to keep. As I walked into the dining room, the floor cried of dirt and old coins. Alone, I bent down to pick up the coins.

It was then the Holy Spirit's voice overcame my mind. He spoke clear and directly to my spirit. He whispered to me, "You will gain riches here, my daughter." I knew immediately what He meant. When we earn money, work is involved. People rarely win the lottery, rather work hard for the things they earn. He was already preparing me for what was ahead.

I swept the coins into a dustpan and emptied them into a bowl. I walked from room to room praying out blessings. Crying out for his presence to dwell there. I was happy. I was expectant. My eyes gazed into the joyful dream of years raising my family there. This 200-year-old farmhouse was in desperate need of repairs. But as I walked up the narrow stairwell to the children's room, the sun shone bright through the upstairs window onto my face. I felt the warmth of his presence as I took in the faint smell of pine and old memories that lingered there. I felt the heritage as I continued to walk up the stairs. Slowly I went, savoring each step to the top. Adventure welled up in my soul as I rounded the corner to the bedroom.

My expectant and hopeful heart smiled. I was home. My dream was coming true as I sat on the dusty floor below me. I stood up and looked out the window of the second story room. I watched the river dance along the valley of the farm-land. I was high on his love for me. I gazed upon the old mill and the beauty and productivity it once had.

With the window open, a cool breeze wafted through the room. Again the Holy Spirit spoke to my heart. Even in all my excitement, I knew what he was saying. It was as if I knew this was too good to be true. I blew off his advice even before he spoke it. That place was my dream. Surely it was right to move there. All the puzzle pieces fit. As I was convincing myself, he interrupted my thoughts saying, "There's more to this house than your eyes can see."

I took this as a positive comment. Being an adventurous soul, I checked the old house for trap doors and secret passageways. To my dismay all I found were cobwebs and old China dolls in the attic. "I'll keep looking", I told myself. Little did I know it was something to find. Rather, it would find me.

JULY 14, 2013

Today, I was reminded of my charismatic background when God was speaking to me in the middle of ending the duck's life. Our precious duck, flopping around on its last few breathes. How could my ears be open to such revelation in such a bloody skirmish? His gentle and all-powerful voice rang in my ears as my eyes experienced one of the most pitiful and sorrowful sights.

I was enjoying the aroma of my cup, or rather gallon, of coffee this morning when it all happened. Looking from the porch, I noticed our sweet duck. It looked as though he was fighting for his life. I ventured to the chicken coop, finding out that it was also attacked in the night. Three chicken corpse were scattered along the coop floor. Wouldn't ya know it, Matt was already at work and I had to deal with this by myself.

"It would be fine," I thought to myself, "I referee wrestling matches all day, hold down kids all day to wipe up poop and make them apologize to their siblings for knocking them in the head with a baseball bat. I've had a C-section. I could kill a duck. I've got this."

I made up my mind I couldn't let him suffer all day. The poor thing was staggering around so tensely, trying to keep up with the arrogant rooster who is clearly the boss. Don't get me started on my opinion that he is abusive to the women. He probably has several illegitimate children he isn't paying child support for. A man whore.

I reluctantly fetched my favorite knife, the only big one I had and grabbed some rubber dishwashing gloves. The imagination started. I was on CSI. "Kids, stay there. I've got to go take care of some business around back." Looking at what I was wearing, I definitely didn't have the killer getup on. I was dressed for Target. But even then, it was on.

I felt confidence arise in me as I started my attempt to end Ducky's life. I chased him around the yard for quite awhile. Reaching the hill, I was quickly reminded of my lack of working out. Heavy breaths and getting slower discouraged me; but my eye was on the prize. At last, I caught up with him. With my big knife in hand, I grabbed him by the tail feathers and started chopping. Yes, chopping. Freaking dull knife and floppy neck.

It wasn't working so I changed my approach. Picking him up by the neck, I slammed him against the tree. He fell lifeless down the hill. I observed his butchered body not even moving an inch. Then the channel changed from CSI to Dr. Phil. I couldn't hold back the emotion of seeing Ducky like that, knowing that I did it. I felt a little bad as tears dripped from my eyes.

I was a criminal. I disposed of the knife and rubber gloves and thought, "Should I bag these up? Nah, I need a beer." I drank some beer then buried the other two dead chickens into the woods with a shovel . Reluctantly I shifted the dirt and smoothed it around. I knew burying them meant defeat somehow. Sorrow came over me not because I loved the chickens, but I loved what they brought to the land. I loved what they brought to my children. Such joy.

A couple hours later, I figured I should probably bury Ducky. Returning to the hill, I was shocked to seek him flopping around, still holding on for dear life. The little dude was probably quoting scripture in duck language, "I will not die but live to proclaim the good things he has done."

Back to CSI, I had no choice but to drown him in the river. I had gone this far; I couldn't let him suffer any more. So naturally, I grabbed a worn out towel, unethically wrapped him up and tossed him in the river. It was finished. Then again, the channel changed as tears seeped down my cheeks.

I stood there quite shaken up after that. I was vexed. A day like today is a once in a lifetime event. It just added more intensity to this season in my life. Undignified and weary, I asked, "Ok Lord, can this week get any worse? What else?" And as usual, he was quick to speak with his father's love and gentle approach.

"Rachel, notice what was wounded the most in your flock. Their eyes. The attacker's strategy was to strike their eyes to distract them from where their eyes should be. The enemy's attempt has been to change your focus from my goodness and plans for you and your family."

I stood there, undone. How did I succumb to such negativity this week when I needed to fight for an adjustment in my mind? The distractions became my idol without me knowing it instead of recognizing that the battle over my disturbances was already won. Our defender is stronger. We deconstruct Satan's strategy when we are peaceful in the battle. Satan hates my happiness and that the desires of my heart have been already fulfilled. We have overcome this world and he that is in me is confident and peaceful. I just had to choose the rest.

As I write this, I recognize something that is extremely profound and priceless to those who belong to God. That he is continually speaking to us in through every moment and season in life. We just have to listen.

JULY 30, 2013

These last few weeks of my life could have been made into a movie. In fact I'm not so sure I wasn't on a reality TV show. So in advance, I'd like to apologize for not changing my clothes for a couple of days and there's a slight possibility that I could have let my baby eat kale off the kitchen floor. Well, actually I did let her but it was only because it was kale, the super food that fights bacteria.

You know the scene. Tears seeping from the eyes and prostrated in the middle of the kitchen floor all because you said no to a second cookie. I clearly voiced my motherly knowledge, "If you would have eaten more dinner, you wouldn't still be hungry."

Kids throw tantrums to get attention. It's worth it to them to get any kind of attention they can get. Usually the attention they get is not what they wanted though. Watching my daughter sprawled like that brought a flood of emotional motives over me. How should I treat her when she's like this?

I fought the urge to scoop them up and fix the problem. But instead, I walked away far enough to still see them but to show them that I won't react to that behavior. Eventually, she calmed down and redirected her own attention to something else. She had no interest in pitching a fit if no one was paying attention.

This was difficult for me as the mother. I wanted to take care of her problem because my resources were enough to give her what she needed. But I knew my silence would do the job.

This whole week I could have chosen to give Satan my attention. He was throwing a tantrum and taunting me every time I turned around. That's his tactic. He tries to show off and seem powerful. He stands in my circumstances and lies, spits and pitches a royal fit to get my attention. If I give him my attention, I give him dominion over where he is standing. The key to my problem would be given to him. He would have permission to do what he wants to do from then on.

Therefore, I chose to ignore him. I chose to fix my eyes on my Daddy. I fixed my eyes on the promises spoken over my life. Several times this week I took a step back from my circumstances. Sometimes even physically. I had to rest more and my children watched more of the Disney channel than ever. I wasn't a bit sorry. I asked the Lord to show me what would I gain if I gave in and lost it? What would I gain if I gave up?

He spoke and said, "During the trials, I am shaping you and molding you into the woman you are destined to be."

I've never in my life felt more humbled as a mother and a wife. He works so well through humility. When we are weak, He is strong. Often we are required to fall in order to rise up stronger. We become nearer to His presence in the thick of our grieving. Just because I am falling each day doesn't mean He won't pick me up. There is a special bond that takes place when we fall. A trust is developed. A relationship with Jesus isn't all about joy; sometimes it's learning to receive His joy when we feel undeserving.

CHAPTER 2

A cool breeze from the river raced through the trees reaching my face as I sipped on coffee. The screened in porch was ideal for watching the children play outside. The farmhouse was bliss. From sunrise and sunset, you would find me in my happy place on the front porch rocker. Our plans were drawn to remodel the old mill house. Every time I looked at the drawing, my eyes grew wide with anticipation.

Many days of laughter were spent, as our family grew stronger in unity. Our youngest learned to walk in that old, unlit living room and I learned to be open with my Maker. My Papa.

The children adored our pet chickens. They chased them around the uneven yard. Daily hidden treasures were found. Old glass bottles revealed mysterious clues of history. Beneath the overgrown grass were forgotten footprints. I treated my dream home with relish. There was not a frown in my future as I made this house my home. I seemed to come alive like never before. I baked more than ever before. I was eager to serve my family, so proud of my tiny kitchen and small living room. It became my home.

For the first time in my life, I loved a home. But that home didn't love me. In fact everything in that home welcomed me in, only to torture my spirit and destroy my body.

It was a hot Tuesday afternoon in the kitchen. While the children napped I fried chicken on the stove, and snapped fresh green beans from the local farmers market. All was right with my world, silence in the small house. I only heard the sound of the sizzling chicken, and my bare feet walking to and fro around the antique kitchen space. With no dishwasher to help the cleaning, I had to wash pots and pans as I went. Limited counter space taunted me on those days, but I didn't mind. I laid the cooked chicken aside as my phone started to ring.

It was Gwen. A friend I had met through a local mother's morning out group the summer before. We bonded quickly, both having three children. With our children around the same ages, it was easy to talk for hours. Our boys played baseball together as we sat on the sidelines chatting about dirty diapers and naptime schedules. My friendship with her was always very guarded. I never let her deep into my heart and we never spoke of spiritual things. I knew she wasn't a Christian and I was aware of her questions she had regarding the Bible and life in general. It was difficult to touch the subject of Jesus, which is why we didn't get together that often.

She had actually looked into buying the farmhouse at one point a few years back. This was during a hard time in her relationship with her past husband. Plans were ruined when she found him cheating on her and her dreams of owning this farmhouse were shattered. She never spoke much of wanting to live there, only once had she mentioned to me her love for the place. She was actually the one to show me the house as soon as it was on the market.

When we moved into the farmhouse, she was very adamant in offering her help. Moving day she showed up with strange smelling incense and dream catchers as a housewarming gift. I kindly thanked her for the gifts, as I set them outside on the front porch. I didn't want them inside the house, and when she left that day I threw them away. Something in my spirit made me very uncomfortable with the dream catchers, so I went with it.

Gwen was very helpful unpacking our things, as well as arranging the girl's bedroom upstairs. She went right to work hanging up pictures for me, all the while cracking jokes to keep me sane through the unpacking process. She even offered to continue unpacking while we went to our old home to get another load of furniture. We were gone for a few hours and when we arrived back at the farmhouse she had arranged several rooms for me. I gasped as I entered the dining room, set up with our things in the most beautiful arrangement I could have imagined. Her eyes sparkled with a smile as we thanked her, unaware of what that smile meant.

I never asked her to help me, in fact she just showed up that day. I thought it strange her coming to help. I had to introduce her to all my family and close friends. Surely she was just being nice. After all she had spare time since her past husband had the children that day. I dismissed all feelings of accusations and just tried to rest in the fact that she was my friend. She wanted to help me.

The phone call began strange as she asked me if she could come over that evening to talk.

"There is something I have to tell you, it cannot wait. It has to do with your house."

My mind raced, palms sweated, as I knew I was up for a battle. I knew that she was not intentionally coming over to hurt me. But this wouldn't be easy. We have very different views on Christianity and new age practices. After all I didn't even know this woman very personally. I was blindly inviting her into our home, yet again. Except this time I could be prepared. I prayed through dinner, hardly even eating a bite. With my husband Matt still working late, I laid the kids in bed alone, ribs tightening from stress.

Trembling with fear, I imagined her words about our house as I leaned over the sink scrubbing dishes that night. My spirit felt trouble was on its way.

AUGUST 5, 2013

Being a landscaper's wife, the Lord uses metaphors about nature to speak wisdom to me. I always love it when He speaks to me indirectly to make me seek and ponder on it. It drives me to go deeper with Him and know His ways, even in the times when opposition is thrown my way.

Not long before I met Matt, my husband, the Lord offered me a precise verse in the Bible concerning my life. At that time, I had just left a verbally abusive and manipulative relationship with an older guy. I sat on an old chair at a youth retreat and I opened my Bible. God gave me a verse as if it was the most valuable gift anyone could give.

Ecclesiastes 3:1-2
For everything there is a season, and a time for every matter under heaven:
a time to be born, and a time to die;
a time to plant, and a time to pluck up what is planted

It was only a few short weeks later that I met Matt that this verse rang inside of me. The old me was dying and the new me, the real me, was coming alive. Before, I was in a season of rebellion. But seasons just don't last.

In my life, I've come to realize something critical that people must do. To really flourish in the next season in life, we must be pruned. Just as a bush needs to be trimmed in order to grow bigger, our lives should be pruned in order to grow bigger. For a while the plant may seem lifeless and naked after it's trimmed. We think, maybe it should just be cut down. But if we could see the beautiful fruit and eye-catching blooms before they even come, then it would be much easier to get through the season of pruning.

If you look into that chapter further, it should awaken your thoughts on life. It should give you hope.

a time to kill, and a time to heal;
a time to break down, and a time to build up;
a time to weep, and a time to laugh;
a time to mourn, and a time to dance;
a time to cast away stones, and a time to gather stones together;
a time to embrace, and a time to refrain from embracing;
a time to seek, and a time to lose;
a time to keep, and a time to cast away;
a time to tear, and a time to sew;
a time to keep silence, and a time to speak;
a time to love, and a time to hate;
a time for war, and a time for peace.

Pruning hurts, definitely when things I am attached to are cut off. My car. My house. My job. It also hurts my pride and brings me to my knees. But I know that I'm not alone in this season. Jesus is right along side me. He's speaking and loving on me.

Another thing I've learned is that pruning is necessary for the introduction of a season of greatness. How can I be prepared for the great things of God if I'm not stripped of dead and lifeless attachments?

I'm learning that saving my pride is worthless. We all fall short. We all make mistakes. When we admit we need help, we open the door for his spirit to come in and rearrange. It always turns out better this way.

I've been asking Jesus to guard my heart and mind in this distressing season of my life. I believe he is helping me change my mind from being burdened by disappointment and disbelief into being enlightened by joy and peace. He is a good Daddy. His plans for my family and me are good. Actually they are better than good.

AUGUST 15, 2013

As much as I hate to say it, childbirth just isn't what I always dreamed of. I think about the many women who are silent, quietly nodding their heads while they wipe their angry tears. Every woman deeply longs to have a peaceful, tranquil and spiritual birth. Maybe their first birth was traumatic and they refuse to do it again. To be disappointed again with no hope.

Actually, I've been where they are. Struggling with postpartum depression. Feeling empty and alone. Struggling to bond with my baby. Now looking back, I'd like to tell other mothers that it will surely pass. They will be whole again.

I've written my daughters birth story before, but with her first birthday coming up I feel such intensity to write about the first year of her precious life. She was made for me to love. Jesus knew the whole time I would come through. But he also used this dark time in my life to love me and to show me exactly who he was, that he is faithful. He romanced me in ways that I can't explain in words, but I will try.

I heard from a friend today that she was struggling with PPD and she asked me to pray. Listening to her struggle for overcoming the hurt and trauma was overwhelming me with grief for her. It took me back almost a year ago to the intense anger I felt towards my body and God. I had to share it with women I don't personally know but that I love. I know their struggles and the dark they are hiding behind, with a smile masking their face. They are gasping for air, as I was.

For these women, I pray for daily and just want to wrap my arms around them and let them cry for what could have been. Let them be angry. Let them process that anger. My ears would be open to them because it was something I had to deal with and wrestle between my Father and me. And boy, did we wrestle. Have I ever mentioned before that I am stubborn?

As a Christian woman I had it ingrained in my mind that I needed to have joy in all things and I needed to suck it up and get over my hurt and move on. I needed to be overjoyed in the fact that I had a healthy child. Let me tell you, I was. I was over the moon grateful that the Lord saved Adah like he did. Actually, she could have died. In the process of me birthing her, I could have also died. My husband could have lost his high school sweetheart and mother of his children right before his eyes. How could I have been so selfish to fall under this depression?

I struggled with lies since she was placed on my chest at 7:10 pm. My body was worthless. God didn't see me as strong enough to birth at home. I would have given up anyway. My body was too small to birth her. In fact, I've never felt so small in my life. I have every flaming arrow aimed for my mind and self esteem. The illusion was that I thought they were true, not realizing they were arrows that had already gone deep within me.

I was so stubborn that once my two-week mark was up to drive, I was already out going around town. I was super mom! I totally ignored the fact that I was completely dead inside. I had no feelings towards anyone. I was moving on with life as a corpse, slain and foul.

I stopped talking to the Lord. I was mad as hell. There's really no other way to describe it. I thought he ripped my life long dream away. I knew that it was ok to be aggravated with God. He isn't going to strike you with lightening or kill your Momma. He knows because He also went through it in a garden called Gethsemane. He loves you through it.

I put on a beautiful mask. I got my hair done. I shopped for new clothes. I made up new recipes. I tried to find my self worth in being intimate with my husband. But nothing worked. Nothing would have ever worked, but laying my hurt at the cross.

One Sunday at church, I went up to the front for prayer. Adah was around 6 months old at this time. I couldn't mask my life anymore. I couldn't live in the lie that I was a happy mother of three. I was a miserable mother of three. I still pray to this day that they weren't affected by my hateful, selfish attitude. I pray that they will forgive me.

I stood at the altar as someone prayed for me. I was as cold as a stone but I knew I had to do something for the sake of my family. The person ministering to me immediately started speaking joy over me. Joy? How could I have joy when I was so ticked off? Then something clicked in my heart.

During that prayer I realized that I was human. That's seems simple, right? But to me it was liberating. I was free to cry and free to be disappointed, angry and question what I believe in for a season.

So, that I did. I questioned my faith and wrestled with my Daddy for a year. He showed me relentlessly how romantic he is. How he loves to woo me in the midst of my anger. He softens my features to make my smile genuine, not plastic.

He loves me so much that in this year of confusion and anger he gave me the home of my dreams. He gave me a home that for once in my life I feel at peace. When I walk in the door, a natural smile comes across my face. He wasn't mad at me for being mad at him. He loved me through it all. He walked me down the aisle to my destiny.

Every time I walk outside on this land I feel such expectancy for the things to come. I feel like everything worked out to glorify Him. He loves me despite my flaws and selfishness. He loves me when I'm kicking and screaming like a child.

The bond between Adah and I has been absolutely amazing and profound. She has rocked my world to my core. Her sweet disposition has softened and fashioned me into a much more patient and steadfast mother. My bond with her is more than I could have ever asked for. She will breast feed until she goes to college and, if I am still producing, she can continue after she gets married. That's not weird is it?

In my eyes, Adah will forever be my sweet baby that transformed my life. What a blessing she is. What a light in my darkness. She guided me out with her smile. She guided me out with the cute way she wrinkles her nose. She guided me out with the way she loves on her big brother. She guided me out with the way she lights up when daddy gets home. She is a light. She brought me joy when I refused it.

Her middle name is Harbor. And yes, she was my Harbor in my storm.

CHAPTER 3

The knock on the front door sent chills down my spine. Opening the door, I struggled to find the words to greet her. Deep breaths of apprehension overcome my lungs as I invited her in. She had a big smile on her face as she entered the house, but I knew this wasn't a friendly visit. I could feel in my spirit that something evil was brewing. My once peaceful house became shaky as she entered the front door. It was no longer mine but I became a prisoner to the four crumbling walls.

My first panic attack happened right there in my kitchen. I knew exactly what was happening as my ribs gasped for air. I was able to calm myself enough to show her into the living room.

Wine bottle in hand and jokes about sipping it until it was gone rang around the room. I journeyed into the living room that she was acquainted with so personally. The surprise in her voice as she complemented me on my decorating skills barely made it to my ears. I was listening to the Holy Spirit. I beckoned him to speak through my lips, to protect my sleeping children and to guard my heart.

Her hands caressed the walls as she complimented its wood finish. The vintage feel of the home drew her in she said. The floor soaked in the living room lamp as it reflected beams of light. The floors were so worn and old that if you looked closely you could see the ground. I had overlooked this detail in my awe of its beauty. We would put in new floors later, but for that season I relished it's beauty.

We walked out onto the front porch; a cool breeze sent a chill down my spine as two rockers were pulled together and the wine was poured. White and cold, just as I like it in late August. We sat in silence for a moment as she sipped on her wine. I wanted to devour the glass but I remained careful. Whatever she was going to say I needed to be fully there. Fully armed.

She sipped and we sat in pure silence. Like a chess game, waiting to see if your opponent would make the first move. I rocked and our eyes met. I quickly looked away as to not seem anxious.

Just then something rustled in the front yard. She jumped out of her seat to look. Knowing that it was nothing serious, I observed her behavior. I could tell by her movements she had already been drinking. Perhaps her guilt was overcoming her for what she had done in my home.

Thoughts stormed through my mind. "What could she have possibly done to provoke my spirit in such a way? Spiritual walls that seemed so secure are now crumbling before me."

AUGUST 23, 2013

The day after you almost went into shock from having a body temperature that of a homeless alcoholic in 28 degree weather, you think about the important things in life. Like, are my kids pooping regularly? Why does black coffee taste like a dirty diaper? Is fluoride killing my thyroid?

Yesterday was a normal day. Rhema got her hair caught in a magazine stand holder for 17 hours. Asher looked for just one shoe, in agony, while yelling at his sister to get in the car. Adah nursed all day and was completely content to hang out on my hip and suck on pita chips.

I had a parent and teacher's conference at Asher's school. I cried a little during the conference when his teacher prayed favor over our family and cried more when she handed me a tissue and told me I was doing the best I can. I cried because I was overwhelmed with stress and anxiety that I was blinded to how everyone else viewed me. Capable. Then we went out for lunch with the kids and my aunt. Coming home, I knew I had to prepare dinner but somehow ended with me only giving them cheese sticks and fruit snacks. I felt off, really off.

Asher came inside from helping Rhema on the trampoline. I found myself sulking on the kitchen floor, cold and weak.

"Momma, are you sick?"

"Pray for me, buddy."

"Jesus I pray you would heal Mommas tummy. Amen."

He knew.

I asked him to get my phone. Adah was crying for me in the living room but I couldn't move. I was frozen. Everything was a blur. I attempted to make a few phone calls, trying to remain calm. Something bad was happening and

I was alone with my three babies. Asher helped by finding the thermometer. It read 94.6.

Am I dying? I made my way over to the fireplace and told Asher that momma was cold. He got me several blankets and covered me. He then got me a cup of hot water. I was shaking in fear, moving around in panic. He prayed again and this time Rhema joined in. All I could think about was passing out in front of my children. The only word I could say aloud was, "Jesus. Jesus."

Is that not all we need to say when we need him? Don't my children call my name when they need me? Won't he answer?

Yes.

News got to my father-in-law because Matt was an hour away at a job site. He came in and I knew I was safe now. He lifted me onto the sofa and gathered more blankets to cover me. But all of the sudden, something happened and I couldn't move. I could barely breathe but I was still able to call on the Lord. The prayers of my father-in-law became louder and more forceful. I felt something break off and rest filled my body.

Minutes later my mom arrived and they both carried me to her car. I could hear Adah crying in the house and Rhema asking where I was going. I had to leave my nursing baby. My heart stayed with them.

Riding in the car to the hospital, I started sobbing uncontrollably. I'm not a huge crier but I felt Jesus doing something. I felt His presence in the midst of what I know the enemy wanted to harm. The peace of God overshadowed us.

We waited in the ER for three hours. My mom prayed over me and comforted me, teaching me how to breathe. Matt finally arrived and as he walked in, my anxiety fell to the ground. He is my helper and he'll always be.

I couldn't walk so I had to be wheeled back and forth to do blood work from the bathroom to the steam room the pedicure room. I had to use the bathroom a thousand times. Matt wheeled me along saying, "Come on Margaret!"

See, that's why I married him. We don't take life too seriously, only Jesus. We might as well have fun. I laughed until I hurt. Well, I was hurting already. Finally we got a room. It was a nice date night. I got to wear one of those sexy hospital gowns and have blood drawn. We watched endless amounts of PBS and I learned how to make my own whiskey. Now I'll be getting on that ASAP.

The doctor came in the room. "You aren't pregnant are you?"

"No I have three at home. There better not be one hanging out in there. Although there might be; I get pregnant if he just looks at me funny."

The doctor wasn't amused at our humor. I'll pray for her.

"No gall stones. Blood work came back normal. I think you need to see a GI specialist."

We enjoyed our stay at the hospital lodge but I had to get home. I had to nurse someone, anyone! I was about to go up to the 5th floor and find an exhausted new mother and offer myself as a wet nurse. You sleep dear. This kid won't know the difference.

What did I conclude from this? Toothpaste, coffee and wine all contain fluoride. I consume all of them on a regular basis. Especially toothpaste, you know those late night snacks. Don't judge me. After I did some research and got some knowledge from some wise women that that fluoride has been wrecking my insides. I'm done with stomach issues. Done with excessive weight loss. Pass the butter. Where's Paula Deen?

After researching my diet, I found out that fluoride is in like everything I eat. It's poisoning my body. This chick can't afford any more weight loss. Just call me Twiggy. No wait, don't. I swear I eat. All day. But today I switched up some of my diet. I went back to the super nasty TOMS (natural fluoride free toothpaste) and went on a search for organic wine.

Alas, we can agree to disagree about health issues and we should all agree that hypothermia sucks.

SEPTEMBER 1, 2013

Today just started off all wrong. I didn't drink coffee to see if my stomach issues would chill for a few minutes. Well, let me just say that nothing is worth not having a cup a joe. I was walking around like our current government, confused and shut down. This will not happen tomorrow.

Are you bored with me yet? Good. I promise, this gets better.

Matt was home all morning. I love spending time with him. Just kidding. I loved that he could watch the girls for me while I took a longer shower than 17 seconds. He made me breakfast and I got to use conditioner.

But really I do love him.

After long showers, I always feel like a new woman. People pay thousands of dollars for therapy sessions when all that is needed is a long, uninterrupted shower to think and pray. And accidentally pee sometimes.

Getting bleach tomorrow.

After my therapy session, Matt noticed a ton of ladybugs scattered around in our bedroom, coming from the window. I should point out that ladybugs are the only bugs that don't freak me out. They can crawl on me, no problem, but only one at a time. Two could eat my flesh off but one is cute and adorable.

By the floods, they kept coming in through the window. Getting spiritual, I started asking the Lord if he was trying to tell me something. I waited, took a few pictures of the ladybugs, and waited on him some more. Nothing. Nothing but cuteness. I think it just means our house is nearly 200 years old. Any bug could come hang out in our bedroom.

So then I straightened my hair. Another miracle.

After I got Asher from school, I decided it would be a good time to run to the grocery store for a few Synergy drinks and some raw kefir. Stomach problems. Entering the grocery store, I grab a magical race cart and put Adah in her Ergo. Immediately when people notice me they take pity. The looks I get are so serious. I need to have signs saying, "I TAKE DONATIONS" I mean, come on! They act like I have 17 children.

"Are all those yours?"

"Yes ma'am!"

"How do you do it?"

"Jesus ma'am!"

"Oh you know that's right, honey. You keep on!"

"Thanks, I planned on keeping them."

Asher seems to always pick classier grocery stores to say really inappropriate things to Rhema.

"Ew, Rhema! Did you just fart? Do you have to poop? That smells horrible!"

Son, if we were in Wal Mart I wouldn't mind, but you see we are in Harris Teeter.

I grabbed the kefir and I'm sure the lady eavesdropping on the other side of the isle thought it was for Rhema. Gassy child. Yeah, I spiked her almond milk with it. She'll never know.

The rest of the trip was fine. The kids laughing and giggling gave me some laughter also. I grabbed some organic wine. Ah, wine. The grocery store trip was definitely worthwhile.

Unloading the cart was a different story. I thought I had parked the car in a safe place. But apparently, I didn't. I loaded the kids in their seats, buckled them up, and looked for all their necessary items like pacifiers, blankets, fruit snacks and waters. They are always severely dehydrated and starving in the car.

Something told me to look at my cart. It was my guardian angel that goes with me to grocery stores. He knows I need help. He knows I can't handle everything.

Looking around, my cart was going full speed down the parking lot hill. Adah is still strapped in the Ergo. I take off running. Now Adah thinks she's on a choo-choo train. Stretching my arms and fingers as far as possible, I snatched the cart by a hair's breadth of hitting a 2070 BMW. Now, if we were at Wal

Mart I could probably offer cash to cover the damage done. But again, we were at Harris Teeter.

I had barely eaten lunch and I was excited to try my new Synergy drink. Bring it on; momma needs some fizz in her life. I downed half the bottle on the way home. Lukewarm, it tasted like feet, but I kept on.

It's good for me. Gag.

We got home and Asher helped me unload the groceries. He's the best at that. I finished off the rest of the drink. Rhema hit Asher because he took her favorite toy and threw it on the trampoline. I calmly dealt with it. Actually, rather too calmly.

"Wait. Do I have a buzz?"

I quickly googled about Synergy drinks and read reviews about people getting a buzz off of drinking them! So, I quickly opened another bottle and chugged it as fast as I could. There was supper to be made! No, not really. But for real, the buzz was legit. Matt came home from work and asked me if I just woke up from a nap. Boy, I wish I just took a nap. I could go lay down right now since you're here.

Oh wait, I forgot to mention the story about stopping at the gas station on the way home. This is my embarrassing story of the day where several strangers saw my underwear.

I was still wearing the Ergo, mostly because I was too lazy to take it off. I got out of the van to pump gas and noticed I was still wearing it. I hooked up the gas, pressed start and attempted to take off the Ergo without unhooking it. Why? Oh why?

My pants slowly started sliding down because they are too big. I've lost a lot of weight recently. They came sliding down like a 5 year old doing a pee pee dance. I'm sure I made a great conversation starter at someone's small group tonight. Oh, bless me.

So then, today I learned a few valuable lessons:

1: Raw means buzz
2: I need to shop at Limited Too for some new jeans.

SEPTEMBER 13, 2013

The Lord has been working on my "I will never" list.

I don't think of God as a punisher in the least bit. But when we make personal arrogant declarations, the Lord knows it's not healthy for us. He's knocked four big ones off my list so far.

1: I will never send my children to school.
2: I will never have a C-section.
3: I will never own a minivan.
4: I will never get a bowl cut.

As the DMV woman looked at my papers for the new minivan, she noticed that my license was expired. Trying to look like I was shocked I said, "Oh really? Well yeah, it's been expired for almost a year."

I'm such a rebel at heart. I noticed a couple months back it was expired and the thought of the DMV made me nauseous. I put it off for a long while. There I said it. I couldn't ever work in a government facility because there are just too many rules and regulations.

We knew the minivan was the best choice for our family. I wish I could say I was ecstatic to drive off the lot with it, but really I was kicking rocks and trying not to pout. I felt old, which I guess I am.

Rachel. You have three kids. Grow up.

I took my smallest, Adah, with me while my good friend took care of my other two. I threw her in the Ergo and proceeded to walk in. As I was walking across the parking lot, I saw a man standing near the entrance of the DMV. I noticed him eyeing my new minivan. Wait, nope. He was checking me out. See, I don't get out much enough for other men to notice me. I'm not even sure how to respond to being checked out. Should I wave?

His squeaky, somewhat manly voice echoed across the parking lot. "Hey yo! You know where I need to go to get new tags?"

What a gentleman, I thought.

"Um, I'm not sure… Sorry!"

"Aight. You lookin' fly girl."

"Thank you, my husband thinks so too."

I walked as fast as I could into my most beloved place, the DMV. I sat down beside an elderly man and woman. A few minutes later, the elderly lady got a phone call and got up to answer it. Then, I felt the man shift towards me.

"Can you tell both her legs are fake?"

No, I didn't even notice. Hi, how are you? Or. Oh your babies cute. But he starts off the conversation what that question?

"Oh really. Wow no I can't "

How does one appropriately respond to that? Yeah. I don't know either. Well, he went on to tell me how much his wife made in a year, about his eye surgery and current infected foot. He also told me about what he eats for lunch everyday and how many marriages his son has ruined. I sure was feeling uplifted at that moment. I just nodded my head yes every chance I got. Then just like that, after our deep conversation about life and its colorful surprises that he told me about, he just got up and left without a word.

Hmm, ok.

Then a woman came in almost immediately after my friend left me. She sat down in the same seat. She was wearing a black leather jacket. Adah reached over to touch her coat.

"Ah! She likes the texture of my leather!"

"Yes, looks like it!"

She keeps talking and cooing at Adah. Adah loves people, so she was cooing right back as she caressed her coat. About five minutes into the friendship with the leather woman she said, "You won't believe the deal I got on this beauty. I got it at a garage sale for $3! There was mold all over it, but I got it washed up good."

Not long after that my number was called which gave relief to me. There was light at the end of the tunnel.

"Ma'am, just put your face in here for your test."

Can I get an STD from this thing?

I passed the eye exam, surprisingly. So after that long drawn out story, I'm legal again. I don't have to hide from cops anymore. I'm working on number five for my I will never list.

5. I will never get a nanny.

CHAPTER 4

Hours went by like weeks as she spilled out her marriage and past childhood problems. I became a counselor quickly and she didn't receive my answers. She was there to explode on me, rather than looking for advice. Her guilt became apparent to me as she continued to talk of her past choices in life. She knew she was in a safe environment to tell me details of her choices, but when I tried to give advice I was quickly shut down. The subject would change. I knew all this small talk had turned into something deep; she was trying to avoid the reason she came to my home all together.

The pages turned and I was suddenly being ridiculed for my faith and put down about God being the center of my family. Negativity rang from her lips as she overwhelmed me with confusion. I wondered why she came. I hadn't seen her in months, what made her want to come over now? She became distant after we moved and I assumed since soccer season was over I wouldn't see her as often.

The words she said next will remain in my memory forever. Hopefully one day, they won't terrify me like they do now.

"I came here to tell you something. Something I know you will disapprove of. But it was something I did to help you guys out the day you moved in. Just a harmless Reiki thing, but for some reason I felt God wanted me to tell you."

SEPTEMBER 28, 2014

If you are in a plane that comes crashing down, the stewardesses tell you to first put the oxygen mask on yourself before helping others. Why? Well, what good are you to others around you if you don't take a second to help your-self first?

I'm terribly guilty of this. For years I've overworked myself in trying to be the perfect wife and mother. I've forced myself into a mindset of performance and duration. I should keep going even when my mind and body is exhausted. Because that's what good mothers do, right? We work, clean and cook until we fall out.

No.

He is tilling up my soil, making me realize I need people. I need help, espe-cially my husband's help. I've tricked myself into thinking Matt needs to think I am perfect. Spiritually perfect. Physically perfect. The perfect mother. The perfect cook. But none of this has to do with him. It's a mindset I've set up for myself.

What other filthy mindsets have I setup in me? What else have I let creep into my soul? What else is poisoning me?

I've had several physical issues for a year now that I've ignored because I'm a mom. I don't have time to fix them. I don't have time to see my chiro-practor. In my mind, I don't matter. "Think about the kids, Rachel. They are more important. You will be fine. Just ignore it. You're strong."

I've learned recently that without him, I am not strong. You see I'm human too. In the name of love, I've tried going until my body can't take it. But that's not love. That's abuse. Do I love myself? Do I love my body?

When we mask problems and push forward it only makes it come up bigger than it was before. I am forever telling everyone else, "You're such a good mom! You're doing a great job. Keep up the good work!" But do I treat myself with that same respect? Certainly not.

I've always put my needs on the back burner, going ahead to prepare everyone else's meals. I've been cruel to my mind and my body. In order to keep on, I need me time. I need time with my Father. I need to be fed. I need to be healthy. I need to receive love.

So I think I'll start today. I'll receive love and help from my husband. I'll receive love and help from my family. And mostly, I'll receive from my father. What does he wish to tell me today? How many times has he told someone to give me a prophetic word like, "You're a good mother! You're a great wife. You will do great things." Did I ever believe those words from God? Rather, it only pushed me to try harder to live up to those words. But I never realized that God was simply saying that I was already enough.

I tried harder. Stayed up later. Got up earlier. I was a slave driver to myself. But no more. I'm tired.

OCTOBER 1, 2013

Please, let me be the first to say that inspirational quotes are nauseating. There is nothing worse than a cheesy line that's supposed to make you feel all warm and fuzzy inside. Although, what I do enjoy is to relate with someone else's journey and share a common goal with them.

When I hear a line from someone that I can identify with, it sticks with me. That's relatable. Learning from their experience helps me grow. I love when people challenge me and make me think about a certain experience or season differently. They point out things I would have never seen.

By listening to others, I'm shifting my focus to the good things the Lord is doing instead of giving my attention to the enemy. He likes to scream, fuss and hiss to get attention by setting up traps for me to trip over.

He is the ultimate liar. But would the traps be gone because I focused on Jesus? Nope. They would still be there. I would just be so wrapped up in the dance with Jesus as he lifts me above Satan's mischievous ways.

Wouldn't I be a happier mother, wife and friend?

This morning I chose my flesh. I was aggravated and exhausted from being up all night with a teething baby. Sunday mornings are always the time I get in a tizzy, trying to get the kids ready and out the door. Toys all over the floor, dishes still on the stove. No time to clean. But, I found time to yell at the kids.

"Get your shoes! We've got to go! Now!"

I'm sure Jesus didn't appreciate my attitude when what we were headed to do was be in his house. I walked out the door in a puff. Adah was crying and Rhema couldn't find her pacifier.

At last, we all got into the van and started down the road. Suddenly I started feeling a nervousness that I had never experienced before. Was this a panic attack? I was helpless to control my body. My chest began to feel so tight I started to hyperventilate. I couldn't breathe normally, so I gasped for air. My heart raced and I felt as if I was dying. It lasted at least 15 minutes. Matt had the children quiet down and they all prayed over me. My husband's hand was powerfully placed on my shoulder, speaking life and peace over my body and spirit.

I knew once we got onto the church grounds it would break. And it did. Matt parked the car and I was able to catch my breath, stop crying and actually speak. It would seem mysterious that it miraculously stopped once we got to church. But to me, it wasn't a mystery.

You see, I was surrounded by hundreds of believers. Satan couldn't stand a chance. He who is in me is greater than the one trying to destroy me. What if I saw what Jesus was doing during that panic attack? What if I saw the angelic activity around me, fighting for me? Wouldn't it have changed my perspective?

Jesus always gives the weary rest. I was so weary from my attack today that he knew the place I needed to be, a place where his presence flows so freely. I hear him there. I feel him there.

As soon as we pulled into the driveway of my grandparent's house, my very being was at ease. I sighed in peaceful relief and smiled. The kids jumped out of the car and began playing while my sweet grandmother began praying over me. There is such power when this woman prays. She loves him deeply.

There is a certain order she maintains in her home that comes out of love for her family. Everything has its place, and everyone feels as if they were placed there for that moment. She is the most warm and inviting woman in the whole world. Being in her home feels right, every time. I think that's why I feel so much of the Holy Spirit when I'm there. They have opened up their home for his presence with relentless prayers. When she says she is praying for you, she means it. It's powerful.

To friends and family, she speaks out her notable saying, "Blessings on your head." I've heard her say it numerous times. But today, I felt my spirit tell me to receive it. Satan always pitches a fit but in the end it's Jesus who restores our joy. Yes, blessings on my head, on my mind to see him clearly.

I receive that, sweet Ma Boo.

CHAPTER 5

The horror came in waves like a spouting fountain. She began describing that she invited a Reiki instructor to the house while she was left there alone unpacking boxes. We left to go get the last load at our previous home and we were absent for two hours. She said she saw the stress on my face of the move and wanted to release me from it.

She apologized for not asking me first but honestly had done it not aware of what she was inviting into my house. She wasn't aware of the evil that comes with this kind of practice. She was casual in telling me the minor details.

"We went into each room to spiritually seal the rooms."

She stopped and refused to tell me what was done to consecrate the house.

Dream catchers were placed in each room with a Reiki utterance of blessing. They spent hours sanctifying the house but most of the time they spent in the stairway of the house after seeing several ghostly figures lingering there. They were convinced that a death or multiple deaths had happened in that stairway and believed that the soul of that person still dwelled there. According to their feeling, the ghost refused to leave and started causing strife between all who lived there. As the Reiki instructor was finishing, she did a tarot card reading on the front porch where we were sitting.

Her eyes became cloudy and large as she said the next part. What she said made my skin crawl and my heart make an extra beat between regular blood flow. This is what initiated all my torturous days there. I became frozen in time as the words flowed out of her mouth. She slowly spoke out entering my fragile ears.

"The Reiki instructor set up a tarot card table, mapping out the deaths and tragedies of the farmhouse. The instructor predicted future deaths. Flipping the cards over and over, she chanted Reiki sayings. At the end she got to the last card and stopped. The instructor arrived at her destination and with a whisper yet authoritative voice she uttered, 'It's time for Rachel to come in."

OCTOBER 13, 2013

My sweet Adah Loo, today you are one. I will give you a gift today but last night you gave me a gift that I will always remember.

Leaving your siblings with your dad, I went into our room to nurse and rock you. You usually reach for your bed when you are finished nursing but not last night you did something different. You took time to eat, giggle and smile at me. You took time to hold my hand and pinch my nose. You took time to give me kisses and long hugs. You were assuring me you are still a baby. And all the while, all I could see was you on the first day of high school, your first broken heart, your wedding day, your dad walking you down the aisle, the day you have your first child.

All the while I've been telling you, "Sweet baby, slow down!" But the person that needs to slow down is your momma. I've been so wrapped up in the fact that you were turning one that I forgot to be wrapped up in you.

As we were rocking together, I started thanking Jesus for you, for the life, smile and laughter that you bring. And mostly for saving you!

Whenever I rock my babies at night, I always sing this old hymn.

I love you lord and I lift my voice,
To worship you, oh my soul, rejoice
Take joy my king in what you hear
May it be a sweet, sweet sound in your ears

When you were in my belly and I found out you were breech, another old hymn started coming off my tongue. I would sing it every time I started to feel afraid. I would sing it with faith.

'Tis so sweet to trust in Jesus,
Just to take Him at His Word;
Just to rest upon His promise,
And to know, "Thus saith the Lord!"
Jesus, Jesus, how I trust Him!
How I've proved Him o'er and o'er;
Jesus, Jesus, precious Jesus!

Oh, for grace to trust Him more!
Oh, how sweet to trust in Jesus,
Just to trust His cleansing blood;
And in simple faith to plunge me
'Neath the healing, cleansing flood!
Yes, 'tis sweet to trust in Jesus,
Just from sin and self to cease;
Just from Jesus simply taking
Life and rest, and joy and peace.
I'm so glad I learned to trust Thee,
Precious Jesus, Savior, Friend;
And I know that Thou art with me,
Wilt be with me to the end.

I trust him to guide you. I trust him to protect you. I trust him to love you.

Listen, I used to despise hymns. But the more the Lord puts them in my head, the more powerful they sound. I have authority to speak them over you.

So sweet little Loo, I pray you will love him all the days of your life. Without Him, life means nothing. Include Him in all you do and say. Be kind to people and show them how to love. Loving people brings out your best qualities. Loving people makes your smile genuine and your soul flourish. You are so special in His kingdom. So special in fact that he made sure you got here, on his timing and with his grace. You have changed me in ways I never knew needed changing.

I'll love you forever.

OCTOBER 23, 2013

If someone had asked me a year ago if I was going to homeschool my oldest son Asher, the answer would be, yes! That's what crunchy, Christian moms do right? Ain't no government school gonna teach my child evolution. He won't eat school food loaded with GMOs.

Inserting food in big mouth.

During my Post partum depression after Adahs birth the Lord wrecked me with the idea of NOT homeschooling Asher. "Uh, excuse me." My pride welled up inside and I refused the idea. But He was persistent with me.

"Asher needs to go to school, Rachel. Asher needs to go to school, Rachel." He repeated this to me over and over. "Hush it Lord. I'm perfect. I can do it all. I can make my own mayonnaise and offer coconut oil to a kid screaming about

35

chapped lips. I can sneak kale into a very recipe that my children will devour and I can run a perfect household."

Nah.

I quickly realized I was overwhelmed with maintaining my household. I mean really overwhelmed. With two little ones I tow around, I knew my brain couldn't handle a strong willed 5 year-old. He's an extremely active boy at home with me; trying to teach him his basic skills is a nightmare.

Disclaimer: Homeschooling is so wonderful. I may try it later in life. But not now, and I'm ok with it.

There should be a support group for mothers that decided not to homeschool. We all need to bring a box of tissues and a bottle of wine and dish it out. "Hello, my name is Rachel and I'm a recovering homeschooler. It's been 43 days since I last homeschooled."

So like I said, my pride gently melted away. Nope, it took an axe to get my pride off. I mean it was stuck on there badly. It took months for me just to look at schools. We decided on a very small, private Christian school. I know that I know it was the right decision.

Asher loves school. He loves his godly teacher. I love her. She is his perfect match. He only has a few classmates and loves all of them. For the first few days of school, waking him up in the morning was like waking a hibernating bear. He was grumpy. I was tired from being up all night with my 10 month old on a feeding frenzy. He would ask me what I was doing that day after I dropped him off. "Oh, nothing exciting, honey. Just going to be at home with your sisters. I'll do your laundry and wash the dishes."

Sike. I had so much freedom. I met friends for lunch. I went shopping. I went to the grocery store. For a few weeks it felt like the honeymoon stage. I could get so much done with just two children. It was quiet around the house since my girls are pretty much laid back.

The house has been such a disaster. Panties all in a wad. He's been coming home from school so grumpy. This has gone on for few weeks. As soon as he saw me after school, his whole countenance would change. He was punishing me.

Today after school I decided to take him on a grocery store date, as he likes to call it, to have some alone time. He refused to even give me a hug after school, as he has been doing the past few weeks. I calmly told him he was going with me, whether he wanted to or not because I missed him.

We drove to the grocery store even though it's walking distance of our house. My kids always love to use the racecar carts. It's always a serious meltdown if we can't find one. When we choose a boring, regular cart there are many tears. My favorite is when they are in the horrid cart and they spot a happy kid in the racecar cart. His hands on the steering wheel, plastic grin of his face. It eats Asher alive with jealousy. The stare down is real. The struggle is real.

To Asher's surprise it was easy to find the rare, party cart today. Let me take you back to a convo I had with a hilarious friend a couple months back. I told her, "I've never had whiskey. I've always wanted to try it. People look so classy drinking it on the rocks." She said, "Oh. It's delicious."

First of all, who has time to go to the ABC store? I would have to get a babysitter right? I can't just throw my baby in my Ergo and go in or call a friend, "Hey! I need a babysitter for 30 minutes. I need to go to the local ABC store. I swear I'm not an alcoholic." Well, I just have to face it, it's not happening. So I counted on probably never trying it. I'm cool with that. I have wine.

So Asher finds the beloved cart and I notice something in the seat. "Hang on buddy, someone left their trash in this one." For some reason I picked up the trash. Really Rachel? That's nasty. It was a brown paper bag. Oh! Wait. Someone forgot their wine they just bought. Nope, not wine.

I opened it. What? Why did I do this? Who knows, but I kept going. It was a bottle of 14 year aged whiskey. "Interesting, still in the box." For a moment I wondered if someone was filming me. Waiting for me to be honest and look around to see who's it was. I looked around but didn't see anyone. Then I got all spiritual. Oh my goodness. Jesus put this here for me. He has been showing me lately how personal and funny he is. He did this. He's awesome.

I opened the box. Oh bummer. The bottle was empty. Don't ask me why I took it out of the box. I'm still laughing at myself. I looked further and noticed several empty bottles of wine in the cart. I mean I don't blame whoever had the drinking fest there. Food lion is a wonderful place to throw a few back.

I couldn't stop laughing at myself the whole time.

We chose another magical cart and did our shopping. As we were on our way out, Asher started screaming at me, demanding for a box of crackers I picked up. His temper was so bad in fact that I had to pull over. My first instinct was to lose my cool. I prayed under my breath, "Lord please show me how to love him." I cut off the car and went around to his side. Tears were streaming down his sweet, still chubby face. I held his hands and got down to his level. The words just flowed out of my mouth.

"Do you miss me, honey?"

"Yes."

I embraced him and we both cried for a solid minute before speaking. He didn't need me to punish him in that moment; he needed me to be loving. I prayed with him and loved on him there in the car.

What am I learning? Indeed, I need to make special time with him. My sweet boy thrives when he has a task and lights up a room with his hilarious dance moves. But he is still only 5. He still needs his Momma. Discipline is not always the answer to a child's bad behavior. Sometimes they need to be purposely loved, even when you feel like losing it. Even when hugging them and loving on them is the last thing on your mind because you're boiling angry.

Sometimes I get caught up in the moment and don't even think to ask what the most effective thing would be to do. How could I get inside their head and really resolve this? Realizing now, if I would have pulled the car over in a mad rage and spanked him right then and there without even finding out what the real problem was, it would have still been an issue when we got home. He would have cried more and felt even more unloved.

I'm not perfect by any means; I mean I did pick up a liquor bottle in a grocery store parking lot. I promise I'm not an alcoholic. But I pray for those who are struggling with a child that they just can't seem to reach, that Jesus would show them exactly how to reach their child's heart and the heart of what is making them act out.

CHAPTER 6

The details of that night all ran together as I tried to remain calm. The intense anger I felt towards the spirits antagonizing her started revealing a red rash on my chest. She continued descriptively telling me about the negativity she felt while she was viewing the abandoned house before. How she felt walking around the property, she felt the oppression but yet was drawn to love it. Perhaps she could have fixed it, and brought peace she said.

The property pulled her in and invited her spirit to cling there, she said. She admitted her jealousy towards me; how I had made this house a home and how I carried a strong level of peace. She didn't understand how my marriage was a happy one, even in the midst of raising three children, and three moves in one year.

She knew nothing of our other struggles with the birth of our third child, or the depression I experienced afterwards. She knew nothing of financial struggles we had walked through the first few years of our marriage, but had overcome with God's provision and grace in our lives.

I knew at that point that I should be silent. She was in so much religious bondage, perhaps demonic oppression. I knew my place was to simply be a friend and listen. I held back negative as the rash reactions spread but I kept nodding my head as she talked.

The clock ran late as she wrapped up her monologue. My children started to cry inside the house, which was my opt-out of the nightmare. We stood up, our eyes met and a battle raged on that porch. I was convinced not to lose this fight. The spirit in me, strengthening me would be victorious.

I saw myself standing tall, above her and the mess she invited into my home. This was my home, where my husband and my children play, sleep, eat and pray. Righteous anger rose up in me. Controlled, I kindly asked her to leave so I could tend to my children. I walked her through the house on the way to her car. In my mind, I walked her out with a torch lit with Christ's fire burning her tail. "Get out of my house, Satan!" is what I wanted to proclaim. From the front porch to the river in the back, I wanted God's spirit to reign.

But just then, I realized I was blinded.

His spirit had been rejected for centuries upon centuries. The people that inhabited that property hated Christians and rejected his voice. So He left. He threw His hands up and let the world have at it.

As I walked her to her car, the air suddenly became cold. A breeze blew underneath my lose shirt. That breeze was the Holy Spirit giving me courage to say what came next. Mid stride, she turned to me. Her wine glass was still in her hand. She curiously and surprisingly posed her last question, "Rachel, why are you so peaceful?"

That was the moment I knew I wasn't talking to a woman. I was conversing with a demon. Without a lump in my throat or a hesitance in my voice, I remarked, "Because I choose His peace. So can you. Goodnight."

Wheels rolled out of our property and I feebly walked inside. I sat in a heap on my living room floor and tears consumed my face. Sobs rocked my body in panic as I tried to ask Jesus what to do.

"Daughter. You are mine. I have you under my wing. Not a word left her lips, I did not hear. Not a tragic act went unseen. Call your dad."

OCTOBER 28, 2013

I knew it would happen some day, but not today. He's still so squishy and has chubby hands. He still has me wipe his tiny butt and kiss him goodnight. This morning was a normal chaotic morning. The usual, dragging the two younger ones out of bed, changing their diapers and force-feeding them at least two bites of oatmeal.

"I'm not hungry! I'm not hungry! Can I have goldfish?"

"No, Rhema."

"Everyone is stupid in this room, but me."

"Go get in the car Rhema."

I somehow manage to grab a bra and throw my hair up into a ponytail while scooting the kids out the door. I didn't get the bra on until I was at the stoplight waiting for it to turn green. I'm talented like that. I'm also organized. No wait, I take that back.

I found a snack bar under my seat. Breakfast.

Asher likes to take the time in the car to have deep thoughts and voice them out.

"Hey momma, if a dog runs away and never comes back, does he have a house in the woods?"

"Yep."

"But, why does he have a house in the woods? Who built it?"

I couldn't think of anything good to say because I haven't had any coffee yet. Starbucks was up the street and I could literally smell it. Actually that wasn't what I smelled.

"Adah has a poop Mom!"

We pulled into the school parking lot and Asher dashed out of the car. My aunt stayed outside so I didn't have to unload the girls out of the car while I went in. Bless her. Walking into the entrance of the school, Asher turned around and said he didn't want me to walk him in.

"What I'm sorry, you're five, not 17!"

"No mom, stay out here."

"Can I at least have a kiss? A handshake?"

He kissed me quickly and I went back to the car. No way, I followed him down the hall like a stalker. He turned around several times. One time I slipped into the men's bathroom. He never saw me.

I watched him walk into his classroom and I made eye contact with his teacher. She nodded her head knowingly at me. She understands. I smiled and watched him so proudly put away his snack and greet his friends, which is everyone in the class. Asher is more popular than I ever was or ever will be. I was such a dork in high school. Anyway, moving on.

I may or may not have stood there and shed a tear, but not for reasons that I was hurt, but proud. I was proud of him for cutting the cord, stepping out and being brave. Isn't that what we have been working with him on?

When children are given the confidence to succeed, they will thrive. When we set the bar high for what they can accomplish, they will meet it. I've felt the Lord lead me several times this week to encourage them in pursuing their destiny and purpose. I picked out certain things to praise them for. Praise builds the self-esteem, but actions make it stick.

There's such a vital importance to praise them for right choices and let them see the value of obedience, not just the consequence of disobedience. I'm learning to be active in praising them when they make wise choices. Not just letting them to do what is right, but actually showing them they are building their character and that is praiseworthy.

How proud is the Father when we step out, in faith, into our calling? When we walk out his promises, He will never fail us. He smiles when we take risks because works with risk takers.

NOVEMBER 5, 2013

As I think about the Lord's will today, my selfish desires get in the way. What if what I am praying for isn't His will? What if His will isn't what I want? I'm currently at the coast with my family. Breathing deeper, literally and figuratively. And as I sit here, He has begun to speak to me

"Am I good Rachel?"

"Yes Lord, You're so good."

"Then My will must be good."

I'm placed back on track, no longer will I be reserved in my prayers. No longer will I hold back my heart from Him. He is so good, and His will is greater than I could ever want for myself.

From a young age the Lord had my heart. He gripped me and romanced me. When I was about 10 years old, my mom took me to my annual check up. My doctor was alone in the room with me, examining my body and discussing puberty with me. This didn't bother me too much as I felt like I grew up so fast. Not physically, in fact I was the last of my friends to have a figure, and really I'm still waiting on that... Pass the butter. But mentally I've always felt older than I really was.

Sitting on the examining table he said, "Rachel, who has control over your body?"

"God does."

"No Rachel, who has control over your body?"

"I told you, God does, Dr. young."

He stopped arguing with me and shook his head. He brought my mom in and tried to explain to her that I need to take control over my own body. He told her what I said and she smiled knowingly at me. She knew. He told her that I needed to be aware that my body is mine and mine alone. No one else can ever have control over me.

That was the last time I went to that doctors office. I refused. I had such a righteous anger for that place. It felt wrong.

For years I've been reluctant to pray for His will to be done in my life, due to only one reason. What if His plans for me aren't good? I believe that's one of the reasons he had me trust him in fasting meat for a whole year, to show me that my body is His. My whole-hearted desire is for my thoughts to be His thoughts. But I'm just realizing that His reasons are to grow me and show me his love.

When we really believe that our Father is good, we will begin to see Him for who He really is. But that's not all. We have to learn to receive his love. If we aren't receivers, we can't be good givers.

As I ponder on this mystery, He is having me trust Him with some health issues. Some things I don't understand, but I know He does. That's what the mystery of God is all about. He sees things I don't see and I trust him to show me, because I believe he is a good Father.

CHAPTER 7

anging up the phone with my dad, Paul, I felt calmer and more in control of my thoughts. I made up my mind to face my fears. I immediately took back the peace I felt on this property. Peace belongs to me, although I would have to fight tooth and nail for it.

I march to the front yard as a warrior takes the frontline. It was time for declaring. With all of the energy inside me, I yelled across the property and surrounding ears listening, "I am not afraid!"

I chanted it over and over again. My lungs burned from my declaration. But just then, I began to be taken into a vision by the Holy Spirit. I was in a trance, I felt like I had no control over my body.

I gazed across the front yard and I saw a young black man, around the age of 25. On his knees, he sobbed and begged for his life to be spared. He cried out, "My wife and children are waiting for me at home. They have no one else, sir! Please spare my life. I haven't done nothin' wrong."

The ground was more level then and I knew it was in the late 1800's. Two men in KKK uniforms came up on both sides of this man. With a flour sack over his head they lit his body on fire with large, blazing torches. Their pagan chants bounced across the property and they rejoiced, as he was burned alive. I sensed a tremendous grief for the family locked up in the mill house. Tears streamed down my face. A deep longing for justice projected from their eyes, but their hands were tied. Unable to voice their stance or unwilling, either way, their loving friend died before their eyes. I felt that this black man was their friend, since they were involved in the Underground Railroad and found out quickly, this was their punishment instead of jail, the KKK burning their family friend before their eyes. Other members held the front door closed as they paced the floor in anguish. I felt this anguish watching this horrific act. I had read about this sort of thing in books, but seeing it will forever change my life.

Falling down in exhaustion, the ground let me know I was out of the trance. There I was alone; emotions and thoughts spun around like a tornado. I never asked the Holy Spirit to see the past. But perhaps, the Father wanted me to know. Suddenly I felt violated. Afraid and unaided, confusion overwhelmed me. I wasn't violated by the Holy Spirit, but by my experience. I had such virgin eyes until this moment. Now that I had seen this I couldn't reverse it. Will I have to see more things like this? Can I control it? Could I tell anyone this? Why was I allowed to see this event?

NOVEMBER 14, 2013

There are moms that have their kid's school clothes laid out neatly for the next day. They set their alarm well in advance to properly prepare their little snappers for the day. They willingly volunteer for the PTA meetings and make homemade party favors for their child's 500-dollar party. Thinking about it, I'll probably never be that type of mom.

What I can do is hit the snooze button five times and literally drag my five-year-old boy out of bed and carry him down the stairs. I have the talent of getting him dressed while he is still snoozing and brushing his teeth while he is slumbered on the sofa protesting against school.

"School is stupid. I don't need to go. I'm sleepy"

We finally managed to get to the car and he became a different child. Who gave him coffee and can I have some? He started talking about what he would do that day. I ask him who his best friend was at school.

"My best friend is Jacob. And Rose. And Evan, Isaac and Lily."

Wow! You have friends at school. Sorry, but I can't relate. You get that from your dad. I may not have mad crafty skills but I sure can squeal like a two year old at the sight of a raccoon hiding in the cat food container. That really happened. I thought he would bite me. Rabies shots are against my rules. My rules are simple, don't get rabies or shots and everything will be ok.

I got real moody today. I started cleaning everything in sight. I mopped the kitchen floor with vinegar and thyme. My husband loves that. Not really, he hates it. "Please use regular stuff to mop. That smells like death." He'll love it in heaven, when Jesus reveals to him all the toxins I've saved him from. Then I will be rewarded with endless amounts of wine. Then I will worship, sing and dance all day long.

After my cleaning spree Asher came home from school. Being the observant child he is, he proclaimed after walking in the door, "Oh my! It smells like pickles in here! MOM! Have you been eating pickles?"

You know what, I love pickles. Next time I need to mop, I'll just eat a whole jar of pickles then rub the pickle juice all over the floor. I'll use thyme to finish it up. Don't judge me.

I made pasta fagioli for dinner. Say that ten times fast. It's a great meal if you're hungry, or just human. It's delicious. And why would you want to say it ten times fast? Anyway, I was eating a lovely dinner when Asher came up to me and asked me to smell his finger. Why did I smell his finger knowing that that always ends badly?

"I accidentally got poop on my finger."

Good. Poop is my favorite to wipe off my kids.

Our clocks moved back this week. I just love it! Go ahead and throw tomatoes at me, I don't care. My kids are tired at 7:00pm and are getting up easier than usual. By easier I mean they aren't screaming as much or crying when I ask them if they want eggs or oatmeal. I'd have to admit that getting up earlier isn't as bad because it's brighter outside. If I weren't me, I wouldn't even need coffee anymore. But I am myself.

NOVEMBER 20, 2013

We went to Asher's school earlier than usual to pick him up today. We are well in autumn season and while waiting I realized it was the perfect day for playing outside on the playground. Adah's new favorite activity is sitting on my lap and we swing on the swing set with Rhema along side of us. They laugh, giggle and sneak in a fart every once in a while. Rhema always has to inform me when she's going to let one go.

"Thanks honey. Putting it in your baby book."

Kids are just so creative. I watched Rhema today as she played on the slide. She would rather go up the slide than down. This causes all kinds of tears, scrapes and bruises. She threatens to not be my friend anymore, not eat her broccoli at dinner and even blames Asher for pushing her off when he's in fact still in school. But yet she's still determined to do it.

Watching her get so frustrated with something as fun as a slide made me begin to ponder. A slide is meant for fun and it is very enjoyable when used the right way. Down. But going up is very frustrating because it wasn't designed with that purpose in mind.

How many things in my own life am I misusing? Are there things that he meant to give me as a gift but I'm using it in the wrong way? I'm getting frustrated, annoyed and giving into a negative attitude?

Marriage is a gift from our Father. We must enjoy it the way he designed it to be. Otherwise, we will be frustrated trying to go up and it's a slippery slide. Over and over again I try to tough it up and survive going the wrong direction, the way I see fit. I so often don't ask for my husband's help and advice.

I'm such a planner and a thinker that my mind goes nonstop. While Matt is thinking about tomorrow, I am thinking about five years from now, wondering what our life will look like and if we will have any more children. And it stresses me out, but only because I've chosen it to. I've missed the value of the present.

I'm learning to go down the slide, in my marriage, as a mother, as a friend and with my Jesus.

Slides are supposed to be fun. Let them be.

CHAPTER 8

My dream home and prized possesion became a torture house from that day on. My mind and body seemed to be plummeting. My chest felt heavy and my ribs popped as I went about my days. I struggled to take deep breaths. As the Lord revealed more to me about the property, panic attacks increased. All I could feel was negitivity surrounding me.

Depression started to creep in knowing that my hopes for the house were crumling. Like an old scratchy record on repeat, I kept telling myself, "I can't live here forever. I can't go on being tortured like this."

We tried fixing the problems by going into prayer warfare. It was time to take back the land! We anointed the house with oil and had people join us to pray over the property. We fought for it, but the one thing remained clear; we didn't own it. It wasn't our land to take back.

A frigid, winter night Rhema woke up from her sleep to get a glass of water. I carried her down the tiny steps leading to the kitchen. The wood joints squeaked beneath my bare feet. We rounded the corner to the kitchen as I saw him.

A young boy stood there, between the kitchen and the dining room. In silence, he faced me. He wore a 17th century outfit and hat. The outfit was royal blue and freshly pressed. I could feel an evil presence radiating off of him. He stood there, speachless, provoking me to question his motives for being there. A muscle didn't move on his body. My eyes locked on him as if we were challenging each other. I finished pouring Rhema's water looking away for a moment. I look back at him and he vanished.

The steps creaked again as we reversed the staircase to Rhema's bedroom. I tucked her back in bed quietly and climbed back in my bed. Chills filled my body with fear. Sleep seemed miles away as I battled thoughts of hopelessness.

My beathe became short and the seconds on the clock seemed like hours. I repeatidly asked myself, "Why was he in this house? What did he represent?"

NOVEMBER 26, 2013

I heard the Lord ask me a question earlier, after the fifth time of sneaking up the steps to make sure my kids were warm and still breathing. I kept praying over them over and over again until the Lord gripped my heart.

"Rachel, is this prayer out of love or fear?"

At first I said, "Oh yes Jesus, both in fact." I love them so much I'm fearful that something would happen to them. That's just what good mothers do. They worry and check, check again and keep checking until their minds wander places they shouldn't. Those are the places where the enemy has a foot in a door of our minds.

What we think about effects our actions and relationships. What inhabits our minds inhabits our lives. It comes out in spurts and surprises us. What we dwell on defines us by either empowering or destroying us.

He was quick to show me that what I was acting out of was fear, not love.

I've been really uptight and nervous lately, just not myself. Most of the time, I've been able to recognize that it was anxiety and I would immediately change my mindset, but sometimes not soon enough. I would say something or do something out of character and then look back and realize I missed it.

I've been so fearful in the fact that I've lost my cool with my kids this week. I've never been a yeller, but this week I've caught myself doing just that. My children's reaction showed me real quick that what I was doing was hurtful. Yelling has always been against my rules.

This season of my life is a tilling season. But I've been so impatient with it. Every garden needs to get rid old, dead roots to make room for new life. It's frustrating and exhausting. I'm uncomfortable and tired.

But, there's always Him. He's not tired. He's not frustrated. And He lives in me. Yesterday while fixing lunch He drew me close. I had worship music playing as I do a lot to let the girls worship while they play. It was as if he sat me on his lap to let me cry. I felt such a release in His embrace. I laid all my worries and impure thoughts before him.

"Write Rachel. I have something to tell you"

He does this a lot when I feel much like a child pitching a fit in the middle of a department store, screaming for their 45-dollar toy they have wanted for a total of three minutes flat, something that's not even worth the money or tears.

He drew me up to His perspective where I could see what He sees. As soon as he began to speak, I wrote.

"This house is your growing place. It's small for a reason, to teach you boundaries and also to teach you how to share and grow within small means. This season is to stretch you to make room for more within small quarters, the mystery of the macro within the micro. A purpose of a relationship with me isn't so that you will be comfortable, but so that I can mold you to be like me. I am able to change your family dynamic and atmosphere here in a way I would not be able to do any place else. There is so much activity going on around you but you are protected. Your family is mine and under my wings. In the storm you will not be moved. Look at me Rachel. You're mine."

He will never leave those who trust in Him. He is always speaking; we just need to sit on His gentle, yet powerful lap and listen.

DECEMBER 4, 2013

The fact that I chose not to get wine at dinner with our three beautiful children to save some money should have been a warning sign that I would in fact need some. We always go through that honeymoon stage where we mistakenly say aloud, "Honey, let's go out to dinner as a family! It will be fun. That restaurant is loud enough, they won't hear the kids."

Mistake.

It was past Adah's bedtime anyway, but we were hopeful we could feed her enough food to keep her quiet. I mean happy. Keep her quiet sounds so harsh. But quiet is so good. And she was, until we ran out of food. That kid eats more than me. The waiter comes to the table to take our drink orders.

"I'll have a water with lemon please."

The out of the blue Rhema blurts out, "Do you have boosha? "

"I'm sorry what do you mean?" the waiter asks.

"That's momma's beer. She lets me drink it."

Oh great, that was fun explaining. I couldn't very well order one now. He already thinks I'm an alcoholic mother who shares in her addiction with her three year old. Rhema has started to notice when people are overweight. This is not fun. She was sitting beside me in the booth and by sitting I mean her tiny butt was in the air bending down looking for her doll she dropped. She farted in my face and preceded to say across the table, "Did you hear that daddy? That was loud!"

I pinched her booty and jokingly said, "You're so big Rhema!" Just then, of course as if our paths were supposed to cross, an elderly woman who was very obese walked by our table.

"I'm not big momma, but she is!"

"Here is your bread, can I get you a refill of water?"

Instead of water can I make that a different clear liquid? Like vodka? Is that the same price or no?

I ordered a steak to compensate for my lack of body fat. And in hopes of gaining a pound I added extra butter to my bread. While eating my steak Rhema states she is climbing under the table to go see Adah. Adah was happy as a clam eating steak, green beans, bread, mashed potatoes, cucumbers, salad, tomatoes, croutons, cheese and licking the ranch. So naturally I didn't want her disturbed as she would surely freak out, notice she hasn't nursed in 5 minutes and start crying.

Rhema didn't listen to my instructions and ducked under the table to go see Adah. Listen I was enjoying every bite of this steak. It's rare that we go out as a family and that I get a big juicy steak with A-1 sauce. I could go on for days about my lust for that sauce. If Matt were a sauce, he would be A-1. When I fasted meat for a year, I dipped my veggies in A-1 to trick myself into thinking I was eating steak.

Sorry Lord.

So I'm eating my steak and feel a tiny hand run across my leg. I look up at Matt and think surely not here. I mean I know I look irresistible eating this man-sized steak but wait until we get home. "It's Rhema trying to get across." Oh yeah, I forgot. So I stick my leg out to hold her back.

"Go back to your seat Rhema. Eat your dinner."

"No, no, no!"

So I held my leg there with her squirming while I'm thinking of the perfect opening line to my mother of the year speech. If you looked at me from another table you would have thought, "Oh look how peaceful that mother looks sitting there enjoying her meal with her family. She isn't even breaking a sweat." Well, the sweat was in my leg trying to wrestle her underneath the table.

She escaped and I had to finally deal with it. I put her back in her seat and that resulted in tears. Then Rhema started crying. "I have to pee pee Momma!" Oh good, I do too with all that water I drank pretending it was a long island iced tea. Let's go potty kids.

We get in there and I thought we were alone. But we weren't.

"Asher honey. Did you pee on the seat?"

"Yes mom that's what boys do. I always do."

"Daddy doesn't."

"But daddy pees outside when he is working. I can't pee outside here. Can I?"

Oh, hi middle aged woman staring me down at the sink. I wanted to apologize to you for that convo but instead I smiled at you and washed my kids hands who for sure touched every possible nasty thing in the bathroom.

Isn't it awesome that even after we are loud and annoying and rude that Jesus never gets tired of us? He never needs a break or time to himself but He is all ours all the time. That amazes me. He is so patient and kind. He doesn't ever get frustrated with me or anyone else. He always orders water.

DECEMBER 9, 2013

Yesterday I woke up with a weight on my chest. I felt heavier, even physically. I felt a yoke and burden overwhelming me. I went about my day, praying aloud while changing diapers, making lunch and doing my usual housework. My kids are used to this and by now they pray with me.

"Mom, you talking to Jesus?"

"Yes, wanna talk to him with me?"

I had a fabulous plan to make a Hello Kitty cake for Rhema's birthday party. It was her birthday and I wanted to make it exceptional for her. I had it all in my head, how it was going to look and taste and how her precious face would light up when she blew out her candles. I wanted the cake to be as special as she is. Oh, she's so special.

Out of nowhere, I began to have a series of panic attacks again. The first one, I was able to breathe through it and pray aloud. All I could get out of my mouth was the most powerful word of all, Jesus! My physical body was experiencing trauma and fear but my mind was in a different place. I was seated with Him, on His lap. I had peace and joy. It was mine for the taking, because I'm His daughter. I didn't have to agree with what was trying to take over my body. So I chose peace.

When you stop paying attention to a child that is screaming for his fifth cookie of the night, won't he stop? Doesn't he eventually understand that his tantrum isn't working? That is what I chose to do with Satan. I refused to give him my attention, and he stopped. Breath came back to me and I simply moved on.

This whole choosing peace thing is kind of exhausting. It's not easy for me with the intense labor of keeping up a household of five. I tend to daze off at times and dream of the point in my life that it is easy for me to choose peace. Where I do it without even consciously deciding to.

Well, by the time I was physically stable to make a cake there wasn't time to make it. I cried a little and prayed for direction. According to my family law book, it was mandatory for Rhema had to have a cake. She deserved a cake and I wanted her to feel loved.

I made arrangements to just take her out so she could pick out her own cake. As she and I got in the car, it was a struggle to put on a happy face after the intense day. I chose to smile and make the attempt to make myself happy; but in the end Rhema blessed me beyond anything I could ever do for myself. I didn't have to reluctantly form a smile on my face. I had such joy being with my daughter.

We went to a grocery store with a bakery near our home. I kept praying on the way that Rhema would find something that she loved and that it would show her how special she is to us. I was also praying that she would not be affected or even suspect that I had a rough day.

We rounded the corner to look at the cake selection and she screamed for joy, "A butterfly cake, Momma, just like my room! Oh I want that one! I love it!"

I can count on one hand the number of times I've seen her light up like that. Her face was enough. Those eyes glistened and her sweet cheeks dimpled up. She is the tiniest thing, but those cheeks. Oh, I could kiss them all day.

I asked the baker if she could write, "Happy Birthday Rhema" on it. Rhema chose pink, with no surprise. Pink is her one and only favorite color. I put the cake in the cart as I heard tiny squeals for joy. "Oh momma, it's beautiful! I love it! Thank you thank you! Can you move it over here so I can see it better? I want to look at it."

I was in tears on aisle two as I looked for paper plates. Her gratuity for something as small as a 15-dollar cake had me almost to my knees. She didn't care that I didn't wake up at 6:00 am to plan her a party. She didn't care that I didn't have the strength to clean the baseboards in the bathroom before her party. She didn't care about any of it. She was having quality time with just her momma, picking out her favorite ice cream and cake. She's three years old. I guess what I'm saying is that she doesn't have expectations of me that I have for myself. I set the bar high, even when I shouldn't.

In that moment, we were each other's. She could speak her mind without a sibling shutting her down or taking her favorite toy. I was all hers and she was all mine. What started as one of my hardest days was redeemed by my own child. Without that smile, I would still be where I was before.

I took her to get balloons next. She couldn't decide on just one theme so I let her chose several. We had Dora the Explorer, Hello Kitty, Princess and a butterfly party. These were all of her favorites. She smiled and laughed and was completely content.

Tonight as I tucked her in, I thanked my Jesus for giving her to us to love. Everyday she challenges me to love Him more. She presents me with a difference perspective that I didn't previously have. She is witty and hilarious. She is kind and gentle. I don't deserve her.

I couldn't stop watching as she slept. I kept thinking about the day she was born. Her labor was beautiful and actually pretty blissful. I had peace and I knew that all of my heart's desire would be fulfilled. I was having the girl, my Rhema my heart had longed for.

I asked to see her coming into this world. I had a mirror placed perfectly so I could see her crown. I knew she would have dark hair, since I had a dream where the Lord showed her to me.

After my first push I saw her dark head of hair and cried out, "I knew her hair was dark!" Where did she get that since both Matt and I are blondes? I laughed pushed once more. She came after two pushes and landed right on my chest. She was 6 pounds and 13 ounces of pure joy. I sobbed and thanked Jesus aloud. I kissed my husband and felt fulfilled. She's mine. "I've waited for you. He told me you would come. He promised me you would be mine to love."

She was a promise.

During a conference at our church a man was speaking about rhema words. I had never heard that word used before in all my charismatic days. It stuck out to me like a song that gets stuck in the head. I repeated it over and over and was perplexed by the beauty of the sound, "Rhema. Rhema." The Lord began to tell me that I would have a daughter and her name was to be Rhema. He told me that she would proclaim His word.

From the day I found out I was pregnant with her I knew she wasn't truly ours but she was His. He had her heart. He has a way with that girl I've never seen before. She brings such joy to our home I've never experienced before. Her actions, every day, bring me to repentance and point my face towards his.

What my child needed that day was my attention. She needed me, not a party with a bunch of fancy decorations. All it took was her favorite ice cream and balloons, simple, pure love.

Isn't Jesus pleased when we simply love him and when we soak in His presence? Rhema was. She chose the very thing that brought me joy during my pregnancy with her. Butterflies.

CHAPTER 9

A ruckus from the yard entered through the windows and bounced around the antique walls. Peeking out, I saw Rhema playing. She was being her normal self, chasing chickens around in a ladylike fashion. Talking out loud, she seemed to be voicing her opinion about something. Jokingly, I wondered who her imaginary friends were this time. Running around the house, she screamed out Asher's name.

Curiously, I wondered, "Rhema knows Asher is in school. Why is she calling out for him?"

Stepping outside, I approached her to remind her where he was. With a stern face she uttered, "Mom, Asher was just here."

"No dear. He isn't home."

I went back inside, returning to my work. From the dining room, I observed her again. She was still swinging but talking to someone. Her face full of confusion, she got up off the swing and ran around the front of the house to the part of the locking gate. Following her I watched her demeanor change to anger.

Turning around, she became aware that I was watching her. "Asher just left me. He went out there." My face rotated in the direction of her hand pointing out the gate and towards the river. My heart sunk. Feeling the presence of that demon, I knew that it was impersonating Asher. Yet again, it messed with us. But this time it was too far. Perhaps he was trying to guide Rhema to the river. The same righteous angry that I had the night Gwen came to our house arose in me again. I scooped her up in my arms and we went back into the house.

This infuriated me as I scooped her up into my arms and into the house. On the sofa we sat as worship music broadcasted from our speakers. We worshipped and I laid there silently crying.

Emotion filled me. "What had I done moving my family here? What if I wasn't watching? That demon fooled her." I knew that she had seen angels before. But I didn't know she can see more. She sees both worlds.

DECEMBER 16, 2013

One of the most important things you can do for your children is love your spouse. I've always known this and tried to practice it but never fully saw its positive effects until a few days ago.

This year marks the 10th year of Matt and I being together. Three children later, he still gives me butterflies and I love him more today than yesterday. Our love has grown deeper over the years, though heart aches and struggles, mostly financially that we have faced as a team.

Recently, our phrase has been, "We are on the same team, babe." We say it almost daily because with the chaos of life, children and owning our own business, it's all too easy to become mundane and feel insignificant. It's pretty easy to open the door for the enemy to come in and cause division, strife, frustration and exhaustion. Life is just exhausting sometimes. Raising children in a godly home isn't easy. He never said it would be. It's a challenge. But it's worth it, every bit of it.

Sundays are our best family days. We worship as a family at church and take the rest of the day to be together and relax. This usually results in being couch potatoes and watching movies with the kids. Dinner goes from big to-do meals during the week to cereal and popcorn. We throw a few Oreos in there if we feel so inclined. And guess what, it's the kid's favorite meals that I put no thought or effort into.

This Sunday we were, as usual, watching a movie with the kids. All three of them were in their pajamas on the couch with us. I'll be honest and say that I would usually rather show Matt affection when the kids are in bed. When it's the perfect time when I've brushed my teeth and showered, when no one is looking and we are perfectly alone. Not because I don't want people to see how much I love him, but because it's easier that way. Or is it? Or rather, it might be because I don't want to make people feel uncomfortable.

Sitting there, Matt grabbed my hand to hold. I love when he does this. He's so affectionate and I'm so not. But I'm learning that that is how he feels loved. In the middle of the movie he moved closer to me and kissed me. This wasn't a casual kiss, like we normally do before he leaves for work or a goodnight kiss. This was a high school kiss. This was an "Ahh, ohh, geez, why are we not married yet?" kind of kiss. Suddenly I was 15 again in his arms, helpless to notice my surroundings or even care who was watching. He pulled away, I caught my breath and looked up at the kids.

All three were silent, staring at us and smiling. I saw then the positive impact it had on them that we showed our love towards each other physically.

Rhema piped up and said, "Y'all are married!"

It's something they need to see. Not just a kiss here and there or a hug, but they need to see that we are passionate for each other.

Children need to see their parents show affection. They need to see the powerful covenant of marriage, in which God is the center. They need to see much more than that. Children take in more than we think.

Absolutely, our job as parents is to direct them and teach them about the Lord and to be walking examples of Godly adults. That's how they learn and grow. But we also need to teach them at a young age about marriage. Teach them about waiting for the spouse the Lord has for them and about the vital importance of saving themselves for their spouses. When they begin to see how special their parent's marriage is, with Christ as the center, won't they begin to develop a hunger for what is pure and true?

I did. I saw my parent's marriage and the pureness of waiting until marriage to have sex. They openly talked to me about waiting and how important it was. They never once said, "Well. If you can wait, it's important." it was, "You should wait and it's good to wait. You will be blessed if you wait."

And we did, not because they told us to but because we saw the goodness that flowed out of a marriage that had the patience to wait. I want to show my children our belief with our marriage. I don't want to blow out hot air and drill into them all the, "Don't do this…. Don't do that…." But instead I want to say, "Do that. Trust him. Wait. God's so faithful when we do." I want to show them with our lives how faithful He is.

With all of that said, I come to one major realization today, "Don't be afraid to kiss your spouse in front of your kids, even a honeymoon kiss. It does everyone a bit of good."

DECEMBER 29, 2013

I love to talk to my children about their spiritual gifts. It's a way that I am able to connect with them on their level and teach them how to use them. If you are handed a useful tool for woodworking that can do extremely precise cuts but you are never taught how to use it, it's useless right? The tool in itself is valuable to make beautiful pieces and extravagant designs. But if you are never taught its worth, it may sit on the shelf in your garage for the rest of your life.

I've been having some special time in the mornings with Rhema while Asher's at school and Adah's napping. While chatting about different things, I asked her if there were any angels in the living room. She replied with a smile, "No, I told them not to come in because their feet were dirty. They don't wear shoes, Mom."

At first I giggled and said, "Well, I'm sure they will wipe their feet off. Ask them to come in."

She laughed and that was the end of it. Throughout the day the sentence kept coming back to me and I asked the Lord to reveal to me why it was so heavy on my heart. I began seeing myself tidying up after the children, almost all day. It's what I thrive on. It drives me. A clean home. In fact I moved all the toys upstairs the other day so that I wouldn't have a mess in the living room.

Or is it a mess? Sometime in the middle of my cleaning frenzy, a thought popped in my head, "Am I too uptight about this mess? Why do I clean up toys all day anyway?" I fought with myself about it.

"It's for my children."

"No, it's for me."

I decided to be more laid back, and let them play freely. They built forts and I cleaned them up at bedtime. This means more work for me when I'm ready to relax, but they are only little once. I'm an adult the rest of my life.

That wasn't all he wanted to show me.

I've been to several churches in the past that made me physically nauseous. I wasn't nauseous because of the people, the building, or the leadership, but the lack of His presence and the abundant amount of religion. It just makes me uncomfortable. It makes me anxious.

Why are we even here if we won't let him move? This is His house, right? Do we not invite him in because His feet are dirty or because He will get the floor messy and change our perfect plans? We would then have to stop the service and mop the floors up? That would mess up the time schedule the plans for "His service."

Do we really go to church for it to be on His time or ours?

Sitting here writing, I felt like asking Rhema again, "Are the angels in here now?"

She replied, "Yeah, their feet are yucky but they came in."

CHAPTER 10

The creaking of the rocking chair vibrated the front porch. It was the only sound I heard. The river was silent and so was my inner self. Feeble and weary, I wallowed myself in my uncertainty of the house we lived in. I was speachless.

I was only an existance, floating around without a brain on my shoulders. A duct taped mouth hid my voice from the world. Just a wife, a mom. Sure I was a sister and friend. An aunt. A nurse, cook and house keeper. The silence seemed so loud from the darts of confusion that pierced me over and over. It became irratating to the point of breaking down. I had no ears to hear. But then again, what are my other senses for? There, in the middle of it all, I felt the presence of my Father enter into my emptiness. He gave me courage again and gave me these words, "Stand tall. Write big!"

The following day as I sat in that same rocking chair, something caught my eye. Our beloved white duck wobbled across the yard. It was no longer white. With splotches of red all over his feathers, I knew something wasn't good. I jumped from the porch and ran to him, only to find his eyes had been ripped out and the rest of his body mauled. The duck laid in his pool of blood while suffering a torturous death.

That was the beginning of a trail of deaths of our precious animals. Stepping to the back of the house, I found three of our chickens had been fatally attacked. I was struck with sorrow while consoling my weeping children. Other than sorrow, something else rose up in my bones. Saintly fury. Things like that happening over and over just ticked me off. I was furious; not at anybody or anything, but at unseen forces going against my family.

I needed an outlet, a place to express myself; not just with my words but from deep in my soul. I search my heart and asked the Holy Spirit and all I heard were his words to me, "Stand tall. Write big."

That day, I began my first blog entry. The words flowed together like a musical. I genuinely smiled for the first time in months. I felt important again. My fingers were alive as they graced the keys. Humor filled me. I laughed deep laughs as I typed.

The season we lived there, the agonizing grief that pounded in my head like an old grandfather clock made time slower than reality. But all of that grief just washed away when I wrote. I became fearless; a spear piercing my heart and the hearts of others.

JANUARY 3, 2014

The saying "Never cry over spilled milk" should be changed to "Never cry over spilled wine." I understand that breast milk is really valuable because it takes a lot of effort to pump. That stuff is like liquid gold. But after a series of unfortunate mommy incidents today, I need the wine like a baby needs the milk.

Asher is very goal oriented. Give that kid a rake and some gloves and tell him to make a leaf pile; he'll go for it. Tell him to clean his room; he'll go for it. Well not really, that takes more effort on my part. But we are working on that.

Yesterday he saw me cleaning the counter with vinegar and water.

"Ew, smells like pickles. Mom, can I have a pickle?"

After enjoying his pickle he grabbed a sponge and asked if he could clean something. I began to rack my brain for things that I didn't want to clean myself. Yes I know; I'm such a great mother.

"Why don't you mop the bathroom floor?"

"No, that's for girls. Can I clean my play kitchen? Because that's different."

Apparently cleaning a kitchen is real manly but the floors are pushing it. Dully noted. Well that does me no good.

"Sure buddy."

After doing that he proceeded to ask me every three seconds, "What can I clean next?" My idea of child labor and a bit of a break had me convinced. There were puddles of vinegar water all over the kitchen, bathroom floor and dining room. Our house is so tiny it didn't take long for me to wipe everything up.

Once I finished my weekly mopping job, I realized the house smelled like a pickle factory. Matt was sure to gag coming in the door from work. I though, what can I do to mask this smell? Oh, got it. I'll make dinner. We do need to eat. I'll make a pot roast, which goes really well with wine. Just like cereal, tuna and anything else that you can put on a plate.

Adah has been extremely fussy lately. I blame it on teeth, but I mostly blame it on being a girl. She has been moody and irritable, which is probably early PMS. No, not really. But she has basically lived in the Ergo and thankfully she enjoys being on my back.

With her strapped in I started dinner. It was 4:37. According to my law book, I'm allowed to have three ounces of wine while making dinner. Especially in my case, after I took the vinegar bottle from my five year old and he told me, "You are so mean. You're like the meanest Mom ever."

Great. Thanks. I wanted to say, "It's my goal in life to make you miserable. That's why I've hidden the Oreo's from you on top of the fridge." Okay, sometimes in a moment of weakness, I buy a pack of Oreo's and hide them in a place the kids would never look, somewhere high and out of reach.

Unfortunately, my children have their father's keen eye for details that no one else notices. I didn't notice he noticed until I heard a crash.

I had my wine sitting on the island in the center of the kitchen while I was browning my roast. The wine aroma wafted through the air, covering up my hippie ways, as my dear daughter in the Ergo lifted her foot at just the right time and knocked over my over four-ounce glass. Yes, four-ounce wine. At this time it was 4:47 and it was then acceptable to drink more wine than I cook with. And I did cook with it.

Then I turned around to find Asher on top of the refrigerator, Oreos in hand. Are we part of Hunger Games or something? I mean, I know I'm trying to teach you to do things yourselves and work out things as a team, but dang. Screw this. You could break your neck.

"Asher, please get down."

"I can't."

Oh yeah. How would he get down, I don't even understand how he got up in the first place. Not only are Oreo's bad for my children's health but they also have the potential to break a limb. After a struggle, he got down and apologized for acting like a zoo animal and for telling me I was a mean Mommy. We hugged and I took the Oreo's away from him. That was not a response he had hoped for while after quoting his very rehearsed apology.

My sweet younger brother was here through this whole ordeal, probably making plans to never have children while looking for a way to escape out of our house without me noticing. But he didn't. He started a fire for me, as I am completely incompetent in this area as well as a lot of other areas.

He bounced Adah on his knee and tried to distract the children so I could at least take three bites of pot roast. He was a savior in that moment, and quite often my helper. Matt has been working late since this is his peak season of work and I've been a walking zombie, filled with coffee in the mornings and wine at night, if it isn't spilled. My younger brother today was someone I could not be in the moment. Calm. Patient. Kind. He was outside the situation, but in it as well.

Isn't that how our Father is in us? He is very present to help us in our moments of weakness and strife. He is what we are not and He fills in the gaps. He is patient and slow to anger. He is the perfect parent. He hides the Oreo's so I won't get fat and so I won't break my leg. But sometimes we protest saying, "You are a mean God. The meanest. You didn't give me what I wanted." But He just sits back, always hugging and loving on us. But He still keeps the Oreo's hidden from us.

JANUARY 7, 2014

The beauty of a relationship with Jesus means we can always go deeper with him. There is always more to learn and grow in. It never ends. But it is a choice. We have to choose growth.

In hard seasons in the past, I've struggled with wanting to get out of it instead of asking Him what He wants to show me. During my pain, grief and frustration there's much to be learned. In my weakness, His strength shines through. It's a beautiful thing when we surrender to Him in our weakness. He is able to lift us up and set us on a high place.

Today He did that for me. Recently I've been having a hard time to breath. Breathing in deep has been difficult and I've felt an actual weight on my chest. It's difficult to describe but I knew it was due to spiritual warfare.

I felt as if I was in a different climate and my body was trying hard to adapt. It's no secret the property we live on is historical. It's easy for me to plunge myself in books and research the facts about the property without first asking Him specifically what I should address. What is good about this property, and what needs to be prayed over?

About a year ago we had a dear friend over. He is actually one of my first best friends. We look up to him spiritually and really value his input. He came over for dinner and we prayed aloud together. I wrote down the specific vision he had about me but at the time I had no idea the impact it would have on my life.

The vision was of me at a jazz club. I was a little older and I was wearing a sparkling long red dress. The red dress was a symbol of His redemption in my life. My ministry would not be from a tragic event. It would not be from something horrible happening to my family. But instead it would be about His redemption. I wore bright red lipstick and as I was standing in front of the crowd I was singing. This made me laugh and you would know why if you ever heard me sing. It's hilarious. Moving forward.

This was right before I got pregnant with Adah. I had no idea the struggle ahead, but my Father did. He often prepares our hearts for the next season. And half the time we don't notice His huge signals because we are too busy wrestling out of His arms into the next season.

We hadn't been to church in several weeks because of being out of town, at family's churches and dealing with my weird illnesses. I walked in today expectant and ready to praise Him. My church is my family. Well, my family basically takes up the whole left side of the church with all of us there. But aside from my literal family, I feel like the members are my family as well. Worship was intensely inviting today in preparation for ministry at the end of the service. He was clearing the way by removing old mindsets and beginning to replace them with His love and grace.

We had a guest speaker today, a powerful woman of Jesus. She loves Him deeply and we love her. She is bold and caring. After her message she invited the weary up front to be ministered to. All during the service my breathing was getting intensely difficult and I was righteously angry. I knew He wanted me to breath, both spiritually and physically.

I was sitting in my chair, wondering if I should yet again go up for prayer. But then I saw a woman, about 45 years old, wearing a long sparkly red dress and red lipstick. She went up first, arms outstretched to Jesus. She was reaching for Him, hands shaking, tears flowing. He met her there, in her weakness and he made her strong.

"Rachel. Remember the vision? The red dress. My redemption. Go up there. You're worthy of my affection."

Immediately as I walked up, one of my crazy Jesus-loving friends started praying for me. I'm so thankful for her boldness in Christ. As she was praying, the Lord told me to put my hands on my lungs and ask them to fill up. I did as she continued to pray. I asked her to pray life into my lungs and told her a small portion of what I had been experiencing. Smiling, she began speaking his wind into my lungs. Suddenly my body started responding immediately.

With her hand on my chest, she began thanking Him for breathing His breath into my body. It was impossible to stand up. I felt as if someone put an oxygen mask on my mouth and began releasing oxygen relentlessly. Waves and waves of His breath came again and again. It was so intense that I was gasping the air because it was so much at once. Smiling and tears flowing I began thanking Him aloud for breathing into my lungs and for doing for me what I could not.

Breathing deep.

I felt my hair flowing in His wind.

Let me be clear and say that I am usually not the person in a crowd of people being laid out in the spirit. I usually find myself just standing there, not feeling hardly anything.

So today was special for me. I felt like I had been underwater for months and my body finally caught its breath. He was revived me.

I'm sitting here writing this out and still breathing deep. I'm still basking in his presence hours later, because I'm in awe of his love for his children. He loves to show his affection in such intricate ways.

ENDING

I'm the type of girl that hates endings. My husband always jokes with me that I'm just like a kid during holidays and birthdays. I stay up as late as I can because when I fall asleep the special day is over. I carry this into my life, often times repeating special events over and over in my head. And sometimes my imagination carries the event into something much more than it actually was. I love when I have long days to spend time with friends. Catching up with a dear friend is music to my ears.

I don't like when good things end. A part of my spirit gets hopeful for more times to come, which will be just as fun and just as special. Therefore, this book is not all I will leave you with. There is more of my heart and life I want to share with you. Not because I have it all together. Rather, the opposite; I am learning to live in His grace, as we all are.

I only hope that this book has given you a fraction of the idea of how much God loves you. How He is passionate for your attention to His details in your life.

My story doesn't end here. I wish I could say my life got easier, but instead I was stretched to do things that I didn't have the strength to do in that season of my life. You know who gave me that strength? Yep. My papa in heaven!

My joy and well being in this life aren't dependent on my circumstances anymore. Each day I awake and know that if I could live in a home where I saw a demon on a daily basis then surely I could volunteer at Rhema's Preschool. I shouldn't just make it through a day, but thrive in it.

Each one of us was made for greatness. It's our job and privilege.

CPSIA information can be obtained at www.ICGtesting.com
Printed in the USA
BVOW04s1716290415

398279BV00028B/636/P